Lessons That Count

MATH FABLES

BY
GREG TANG

ILLUSTRATED BY
HEATHER CAHOON

SCHOLASTIC PRESS · NEW YORK

author's note

For some children, math comes fairly easily. For others, it is a challenge nearly every step of the way. What accounts for this difference? Is there a special math gene that makes math easy for some kids and difficult for others? Fortunately, the answer is "no." Success is often determined by how fluent children are with numbers, the language of math. When kids develop a good understanding of numbers at an early age, everything else — arithmetic, algebra, even geometry — follows naturally.

In writing this book, my goal is to present numbers in a way that will make math easier for all children. I believe it is especially important to lay the groundwork early, and I have written *Math Fables* for ages 3 to 6. Each fable begins by introducing numbers the traditional way — by counting. How much is the number six? It's a group of "one, two, three, four, five, six." This familiar approach emphasizes size and order. As the stories unfold, each number is shown in different ways. The six becomes a group of 4 and 2, a group of 5 and 1, and finally two groups of 3. The idea is to encourage kids to begin thinking more efficiently in groups rather than counting one number at a time.

There are several important advantages to this approach. First, it lays the foundation for place value, the basis of our number system. When children are introduced to grouping at an early age, thinking in terms of ones, tens, and hundreds follows naturally. Second, it is the first step to building strong computational skills. Breaking numbers into smaller, more manageable pieces and combining them in smart ways is the key to arithmetic. Finally, grouping encourages flexible and creative thinking by requiring kids to think about the same number in different ways.

I wrote *Math Fables,* the sixth book in a series that includes *The Grapes of Math, Math For All Seasons, The Best of Times, Math Appeal,* and *Math-terpieces,* to give kids a head start in math and at the same time encourage a love for reading and learning. I hope children and adults alike will smile at the stories, delight in the artwork, and brighten at the memory of shared times together. Enjoy!

Greg Tang

www.gregtang.com

With Love to Lily and John — G.T.

Love to my Husband and Daughter — H.C.

DINNER GUEST

1 spider waited patiently,
at last her web was done.
Just who would come to dinner now
and be the lucky one?

A fly? A moth?

Mosquitoes would be great.

It's nice to know that all good things

will come to those who wait!

TRYING TIMES

The sun was shining overhead,
    the skies were bright and clear.
For **2** young birds safe in their nest,
    the time to fly was here.

With wings spread wide **1** bird took flight –
but fluttered to the ground.
The other **1** fell from the sky
and very nearly drowned!

The **2** birds practiced all day long
until they both could fly.
Sometimes the most important thing
in life is just to try!

Family Affair

3 turtles living in the woods
were always on the go.
One day they headed for a pond,
albeit very slow.

The youngest **1** soon raced ahead,
but accidentally tripped.
The other **2** caught up with him
and found that he had flipped!

They quickly grabbed him by the shell
and righted him once more.
All **3** agreed wholeheartedly,
"That's what a family's for!"

GOING NUTS

4 squirrels frolicked in the leaves
one brisk fall afternoon,
when suddenly it dawned on them
that snow was coming soon!

"We haven't any winter food,"
3 frightened squirrels cried.
"I guess we'd better get to work,"
a prudent **1** replied.

2 squirrels raced to gather nuts
and made a great, big mound.
The other **2** then buried them
in stashes underground.

All **4** slept very well that night,
no longer feeling scared.
They learned it's wise to plan ahead
and always be prepared!

MiDNiGHt SNACK

5 smart raccoons set out one night
to get a bite to eat.
They came upon a garbage can,
a most delicious treat!

2 quickly grabbed it by the rim
and pulled it on its side.
"We're going to have a feast tonight!"
the other **3** all cried.

"Before we eat, let's first give thanks,"
4 thoughtful raccoons said.
The youngest **1** put down the food
and bowed his little head.

"We offer thanks," all **5** began,
"for each unfinished plate.
Leftover food and chicken bones
we so appreciate!"

TOOL'S GOLD

Along the rocky ocean coast
in water clear and blue,
6 otters liked to swim and play
and look for shellfish, too.

One afternoon **2** saw some clams
along the ocean floor.
4 quickly dove to scoop them up,
then hurried back for more!

"These shells are hard to pry apart,"
5 puzzled otters sighed.
"Try striking them against a rock,"
a clever **1** replied.

A group of **3** tried this technique
and found it worked quite well.
The other **3** then followed suit
and opened every shell!

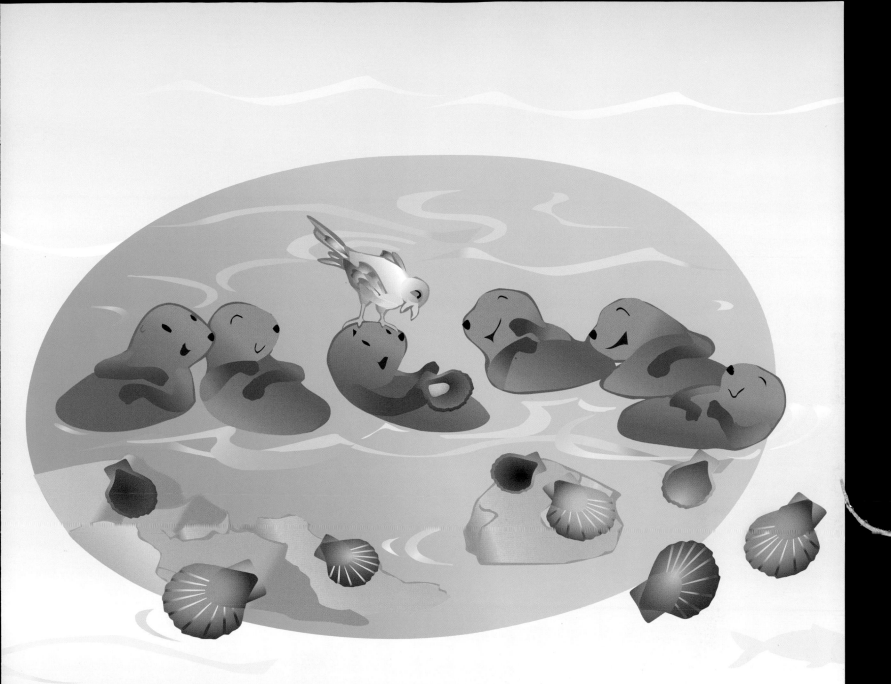

The **6** smart otters were content,
all had their fill of clams.
They each had also learned to use
a tool and not their hands!

GONE WiTH tHE WiND

The autumn air was growing cool,
    the days were shorter, too.
For **7** monarch butterflies,
    a trip was overdue.

"We should have left here weeks ago!"
5 butterflies exclaimed.
"We hate to say we told you so,"
2 know-it-alls proclaimed.

They had to get to Mexico
before the winter freeze.
1 led the other 6 in flight
atop a southern breeze.

Their journey would be very far,
a thousand miles or more.
The monarchs flew both day and night
in groups of 3 and 4.

At last all **7** made it home,
too tired to celebrate.
They vowed next spring to be on time
and not procrastinate!

PROFILE in COURAGE

One hot and sultry afternoon
down at the tidal pool,
8 crabs were buried in the sand
just trying to stay cool.

"The water here is much too warm,"
5 weary crabs complained.
"The sun is very strong today,"
the other **3** explained.

A group of **4** then grabbed their things
and headed to the shore.
The others followed after them,
a second group of **4**.

As **7** stood by cautiously,
1 daring crab jumped in,
but soon got hammered by a wave
that caught him on the chin!

The smallest crab swam out to help,
now in the sea were **2** –
with **6** left cheering on the shore
this bold and brave rescue!

The crabs at last were one big group,
again they numbered 8.
They all then thanked their lucky stars
for having friends so great!

antics

One warm and sunny afternoon,
the month was late July,
9 ants were rather hungry when
a picnic they did spy.

3 crept ahead to take a look
    while 6 ants stayed behind.
Some crackers, cheese, a loaf of bread –
    such treasures they did find!

"This food's too big for us to lift,"
    8 worried ants complained.
"We'll have to work together then,"
    the oldest 1 explained.

With one in front and one behind,
2 carried home the cheese.
While **7** picked the loaf right up
as easy as you please!

The ants were happy as could be
and soon returned for more.
They carried two big crackers home
in teams of **5** and **4**.

When finally their task was done,
the **9** ants felt just great.
They each had learned the meaning of
the word *cooperate*!

RiVER StickS

10 beavers left for work one day,
they had a lodge to fix.
All marched along in single file
in search of broken sticks.

A group of **7** raced ahead
and found a fallen tree.
They quickly gnawed off all the limbs,
then called the other **3**.

"How will we get these branches home?"
9 puzzled beavers cried.
"We need to dig a small canal,"
a clever **1** replied.

So **6** went back and dug into
the river's muddy shore.
They soon had made a waterway –
right to the other **4**!

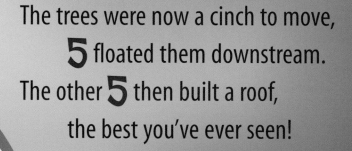

The trees were now a cinch to move,
5 floated them downstream.
The other **5** then built a roof,
the best you've ever seen!

Their home was nearly finished now,
with few things left to do.
8 quickly patched the holes with mud,
while cracks were filled by 2.

At last the beavers' job was done,
and 10 let out a cheer.
They each had earned the title of
Domestic Engineer!

THE ROAD TO HIGHER MATH

The journey from counting to calculus begins with numbers — the language of math. But there's more to understanding numbers than learning to count. The real secret is learning to see big numbers in terms of smaller ones. To help early learners become more fluent with numbers, try the following practice challenges:

7

8

9

10

Count backward from 10 to 1, first by looking at the parade, and then by remembering and visualizing the order and size of numbers.

Find all ten combinations that make 10. For example, the otters (6) and squirrels (4) together make 10. As you practice, use $1, 2, 3$, or even 4 different groups!
(Answer: 10, 9+1, 8+2, 7+3, 7+2+1, 6+4, 6+3+1, 5+4+1, 5+3+2, and 4+3+2+1)

Now, practice making all the numbers by combining groups in different ways. For example, make an 8 with turtles (3) and raccoons (5).

Find the even numbers by seeing which numbers can be divided evenly into two groups. The ones that cannot be divided evenly are called the odd numbers. Be sure to learn the even and odd numbers in both increasing and decreasing order.

CONGRATULATIONS! You have completed the first leg of your journey. Good luck, and remember to think smart the rest of the way!

Special thanks to Heather Cahoon,
David Caplan, Stephanie Luck, and Liz Szabla

LIBRARY OF CONGRESS CATALOGING-IN-PUBLICATION DATA

Tang, Greg. Math fables / by Greg Tang.—1st ed.   p.   cm.

Summary: A series of rhymes about animals introduces counting and grouping numbers, as well as examples of such behaviors as cooperation, friendship, and appreciation.   1. Counting—Juvenile literature. [1.Counting. 2. Conduct of life.] I. Title.

QA113   .T355 2003   513.2'11—dc21   2002005360

ISBN 0-439-45399-2

10 9 8 7 6 5   06 07 08

Printed in Singapore   46 • First edition, March 2004
Heather Cahoon's artwork was created on the computer.
The display type was set in Stovetop.
The text type was set in Myriad Condensed.
Book design by Greg Tang and Heather Cahoon